THE KINGFISHER
First Animal
Picture Atlas

Written by Deborah Chancellor

Illustrated by Anthony Lewis

KINGFISHER

KINGFISHER

Kingfisher Publications Plc
New Penderel House
283–288 High Holborn
London WC1V 7HZ

www.kingfisherpub.com

Author: Deborah Chancellor
Senior editor: Vicky Bywater
Senior editor and proofreader: Hannah Wilson
Art director: Mike Davis
Consultant: David Burnie
DTP manager: Nicky Studdart
Senior production controller: Jessamy Oldfield
Cover design by Mike Davis

Illustrations by Anthony Lewis

First published by Kingfisher
Publications Plc 2006

10 9 8 7 6 5 4 3 2 1

1TR/0606/SHENS/CLSN/128MA/C

A CIP catalogue record for this book
is available from the British Library.

ISBN-13: 978 0 7534 1324 1
ISBN-10: 0 7534 1324 8

Printed in Taiwan

Contents

KEY

— country border

- - - state border

· · · disputed border

river

lake

Desert Dry areas with sand and rocks

Dry grassland Flat, grassy plains with only a few trees

Temperate grassland Flat, grassy plains with some trees

Forest Areas with lots of trees

Mountains Tall hills and rugged landscape

Tundra Flat area near the Arctic with frozen ground and no trees

Ice and snow Places where ice and snow cover the ground

Seas and oceans Salty water that covers much of the earth

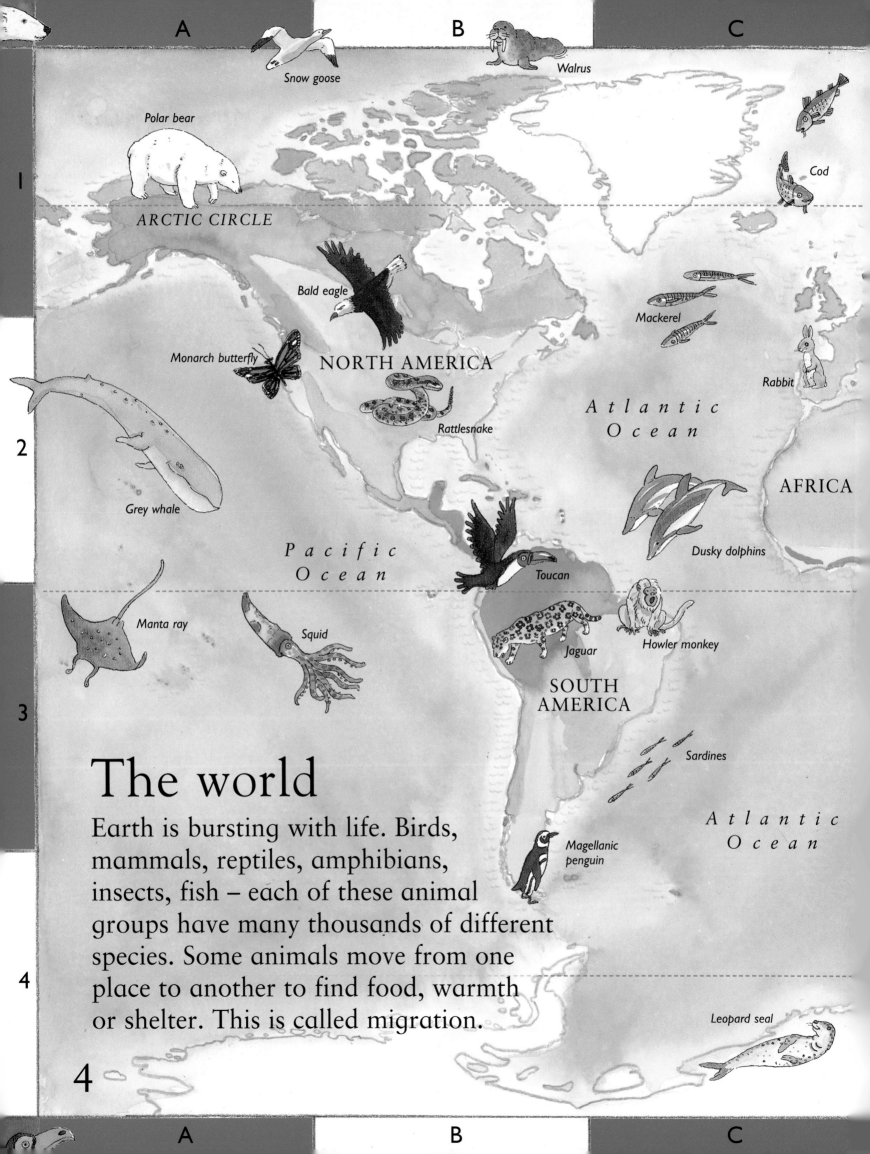

Snow goose

Walrus

Polar bear

Cod

1

ARCTIC CIRCLE

Bald eagle

Mackerel

Monarch butterfly

NORTH AMERICA

Rabbit

A t l a n t i c
O c e a n

Rattlesnake

2

AFRICA

Grey whale

P a c i f i c
O c e a n

Dusky dolphins

Toucan

Manta ray

Squid

Howler monkey

Jaguar

SOUTH
AMERICA

3

Sardines

The world

Earth is bursting with life. Birds,
mammals, reptiles, amphibians,
insects, fish – each of these animal
groups have many thousands of different
species. Some animals move from one
place to another to find food, warmth
or shelter. This is called migration.

Magellanic
penguin

A t l a n t i c
O c e a n

4

Leopard seal

4

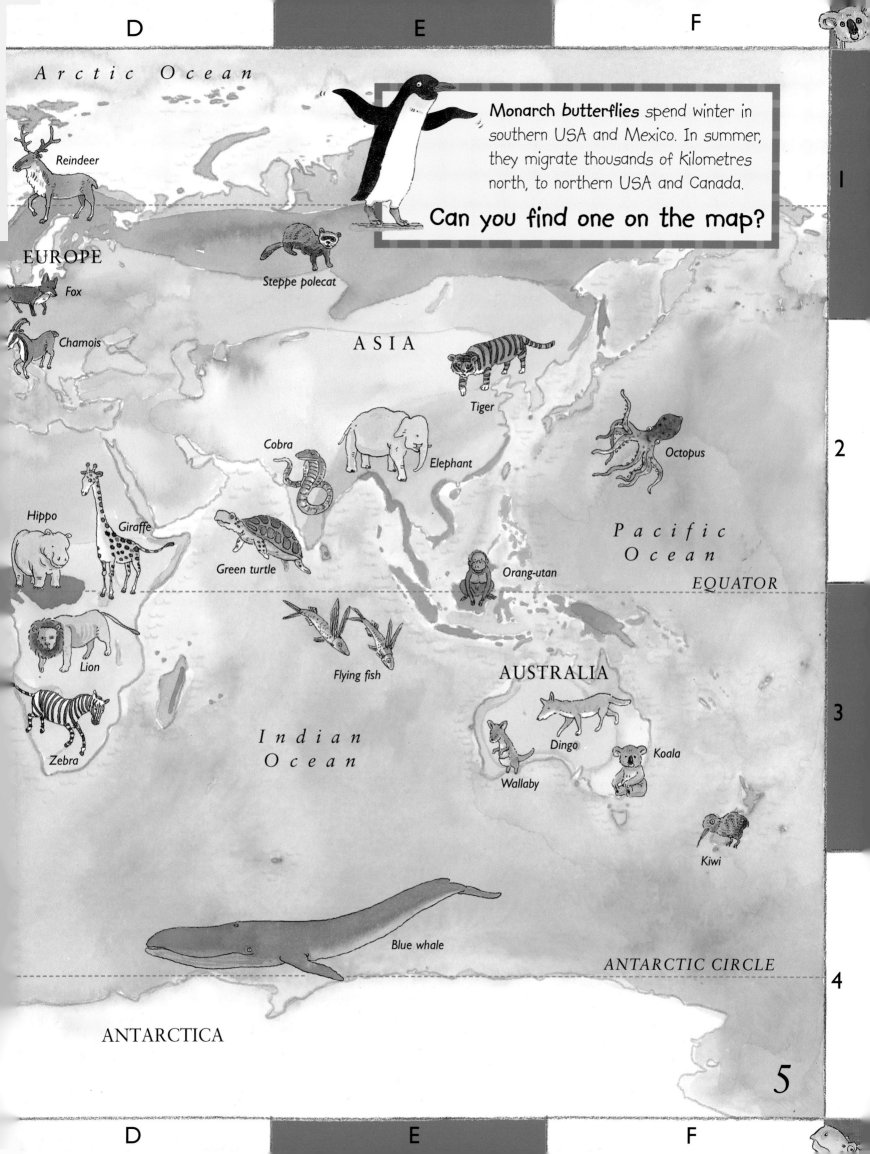

Arctic Ocean

Reindeer

EUROPE

Fox

Chamois

Steppe polecat

A S I A

Tiger

Cobra

Elephant

Octopus

Hippo

Giraffe

Green turtle

Pacific Ocean

Orang-utan

EQUATOR

Lion

Flying fish

AUSTRALIA

Zebra

Dingo

Koala

Indian Ocean

Wallaby

Kiwi

Blue whale

ANTARCTIC CIRCLE

ANTARCTICA

Monarch **butterflies** spend winter in southern USA and Mexico. In summer, they migrate thousands of kilometres north, to northern USA and Canada.

Can you find one on the map?

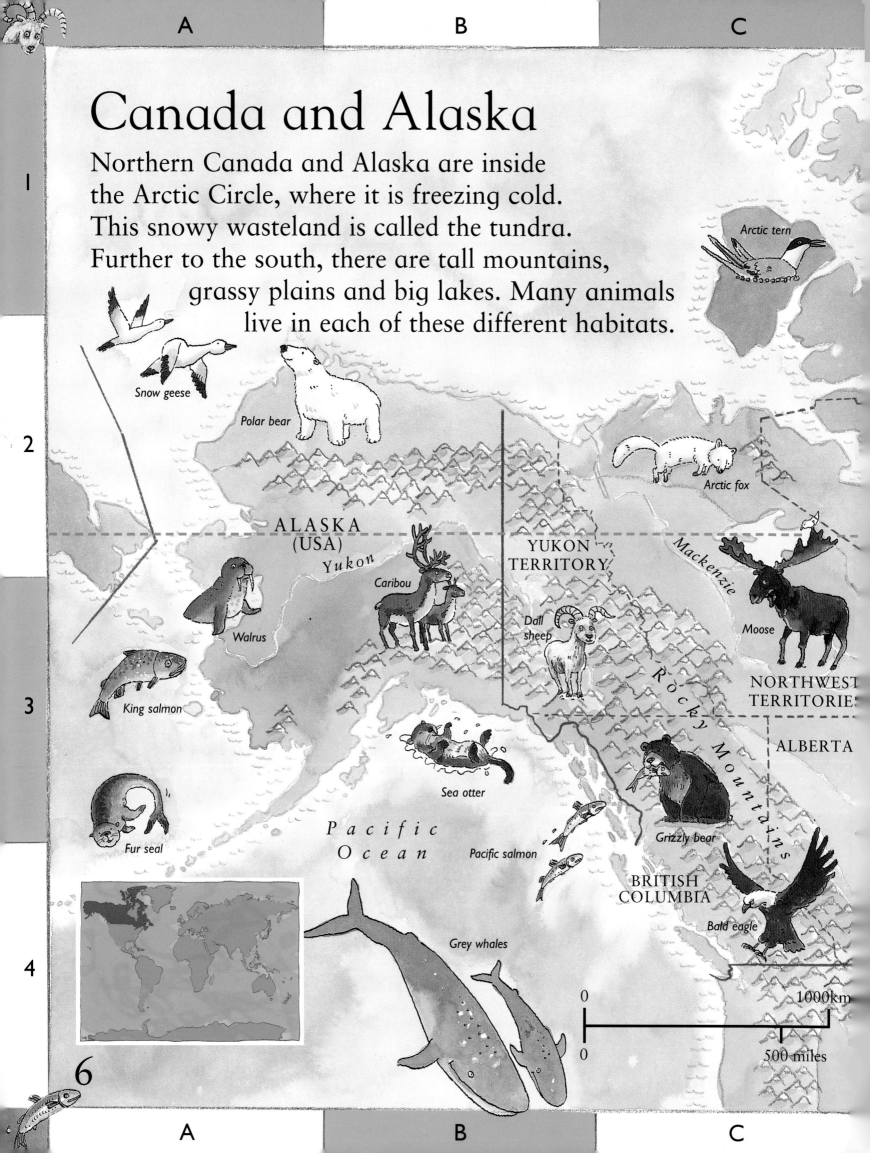

Canada and Alaska

Northern Canada and Alaska are inside
the Arctic Circle, where it is freezing cold.
This snowy wasteland is called the tundra.
Further to the south, there are tall mountains,
grassy plains and big lakes. Many animals
live in each of these different habitats.

Arctic tern

Snow geese

Polar bear

Arctic fox

ALASKA
(USA)

Yukon

YUKON
TERRITORY

Mackenzie

Walrus

Caribou

Dall
sheep

Moose

NORTHWEST
TERRITORIES

King salmon

Rocky Mountains

ALBERTA

Sea otter

Fur seal

*P a c i f i c
O c e a n*

Grizzly bear

Pacific salmon

BRITISH
COLUMBIA

Bald eagle

Grey whales

0   1000km

0   500 miles

D · E · F

Arctic hare

Ringed seal

Narwhal

Polar bear

Grizzly bears live in cold places, in forests, on mountains and tundra. In winter, they dig dens, where they sleep, or hibernate.

Can you find one on the map?

Whistling swan

Musk ox

Lemming

NUNAVUT

Canada goose

ARCTIC CIRCLE

Arctic wolf

Caribou

Atlantic Ocean

C A N A D A

Beluga whale

Snowy owl

Hooded seal

SASKATCHEWAN

MANITOBA

Wolverine

Dairy cow

Beaver

Black bear

NEWFOUNDLAND AND LABRADOR

ONTARIO

QUEBEC

Skunk

Blue jay

St Lawrence

NEW BRUNSWICK

PRINCE EDWARD ISLAND

Cod

NOVA SCOTIA

7

D · E · F

1

2

3

4

0   1000km

0

500 miles

WASHINGTON

Rocky Mountains

Grizzly bear

Green darner dragonfly

MONTANA

HAWAII

OREGON

WYOMING

Mountain bluebird

Horned toad

Humpback whale

Oregon swallowtail butterfly

IDAHO

UTAH

Desert big-horn sheep

Rocky Mountain elk

COLORADO

Colorado

P a c i f i c
O c e a n

CALIFORNIA

Rocky Mountain big-horn sheep

NEVADA

ARIZONA

NEW MEXICO

The United States of America

There are a variety of habitats in
the USA, including steamy swamps,
rolling prairies, snowy mountains
and rocky deserts. Different animals
live in all these places. They have special
ways of adapting to their environment.
In the desert, for example, animals
can survive without much water.

Desert tortoise

Arizona ridge-nose rattlesnake

Greater roadrunner

P a c i f i c
O c e a n

8

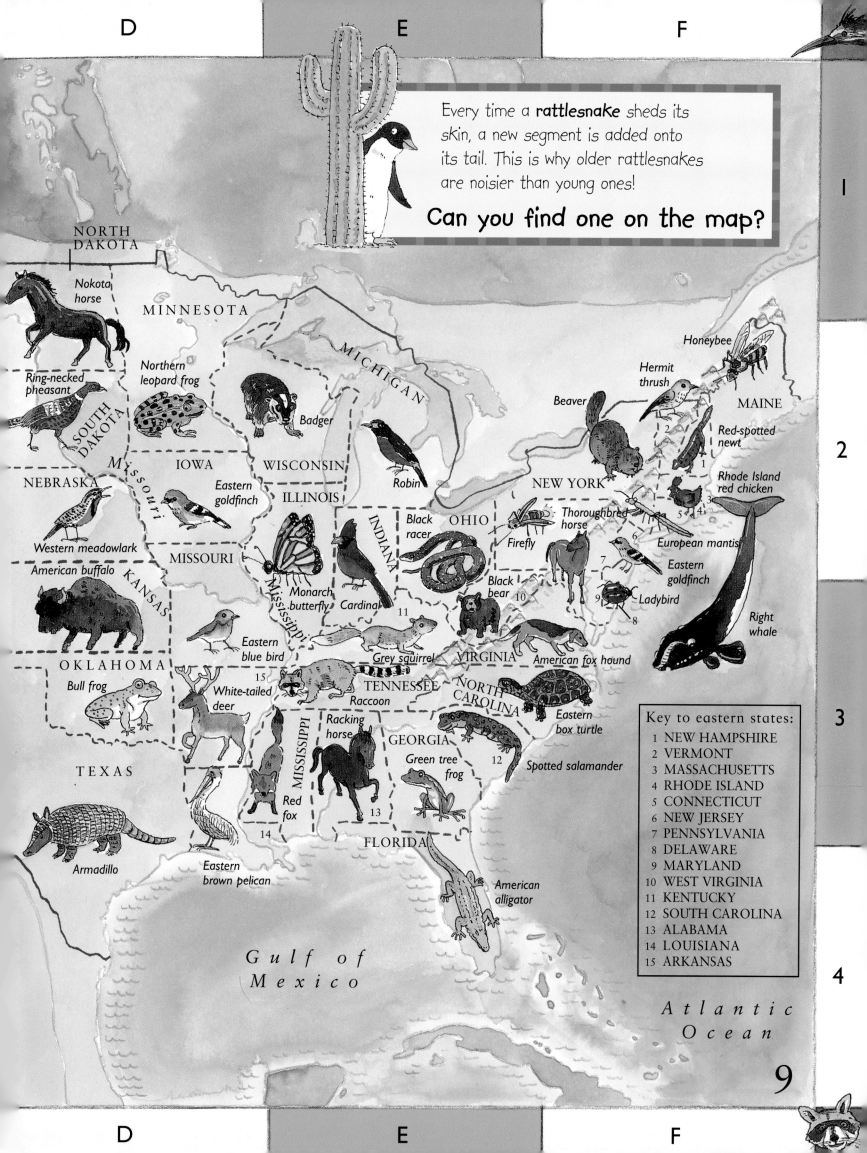

Every time a **rattlesnake** sheds its skin, a new segment is added onto its tail. This is why older rattlesnakes are noisier than young ones!

Can you find one on the map?

NORTH DAKOTA

MINNESOTA

MICHIGAN

Nokota horse

Northern leopard frog

Badger

Honeybee

Hermit thrush

Beaver

MAINE

Red-spotted newt

Ring-necked pheasant

SOUTH DAKOTA

Missouri

IOWA

WISCONSIN

Robin

NEW YORK

Rhode Island red chicken

NEBRASKA

Eastern goldfinch

ILLINOIS

Black racer

OHIO

Thoroughbred horse

European mantis

Firefly

Western meadowlark

MISSOURI

INDIANA

Cardinal

Eastern goldfinch

American buffalo

KANSAS

Monarch butterfly

11

Black bear

10

9

Ladybird

8

Right whale

Eastern blue bird

Mississippi

Grey squirrel

VIRGINIA

American fox hound

OKLAHOMA

Bull frog

15

White-tailed deer

Raccoon

TENNESSEE

NORTH CAROLINA

Eastern box turtle

MISSISSIPPI

Racking horse

GEORGIA

Green tree frog

12

Spotted salamander

TEXAS

Red fox

13

Armadillo

Eastern brown pelican

14

FLORIDA

American alligator

Gulf of Mexico

Atlantic Ocean

Key to eastern states:
1 NEW HAMPSHIRE
2 VERMONT
3 MASSACHUSETTS
4 RHODE ISLAND
5 CONNECTICUT
6 NEW JERSEY
7 PENNSYLVANIA
8 DELAWARE
9 MARYLAND
10 WEST VIRGINIA
11 KENTUCKY
12 SOUTH CAROLINA
13 ALABAMA
14 LOUISIANA
15 ARKANSAS

D E F

1

2

3

4

1

The **Caribbean reef shark** can grow up to three metres long, and is the most common shark on Caribbean coral reefs. Its diet includes sea turtles.

Can you find one on the map?

Rio Grande

West Sierra Madre

Gila monster

Blue-throated hummingbird

Red octopus

2

Mexican plateau-horned lizard

MEXICO

Red snapper fish

Anchovies

G u l f   o f   M e x i c o

White shrimp

Yellowfin tuna

Painted wood turtle

Spiny lobster

Spiny dogfish

Red-eyed tree frog

P a c i f i c   O c e a n

Quetzal

Ocelot

3

BELIZE

GUATEMALA   *Jaguar*

Vampire bat

EL SALVADOR

Strawberry poison dart frog

COSTA RICA

Key to countries in the Caribbean Sea:
1 PUERTO RICO (USA)
2 ST KITTS & NEVIS
3 ANTIGUA & BARBUDA
4 DOMINICA
5 ST LUCIA
6 ST VINCENT & THE GRENADINES
7 BARBADOS
8 GRENADA
9 TRINIDAD & TOBAGO

4

10

Mexico, Central America and the Caribbean

There are dry deserts in northern Mexico and wet rainforests in Central America. Not many creatures are able to survive in the scorching desert, but an amazing number of animals and plants live in the tropical rainforests. To the east, the Caribbean Sea is famous for its coral reefs, which are home to a colourful collection of marine creatures.

BAHAMAS

West Indian flamingo

Rhinoceros iguana

Stingray

CUBA

JAMAICA

Jamaican white peacock butterfly

HAITI

DOMINICAN REPUBLIC

Marine toad

1

Spotted dolphin

A t l a n t i c O c e a n

Frigate bird

2   3

Sisserou parrot

HONDURAS

Green turtle

West Indian manatee

Caribbean reef shark

4

Puffer fish

5

6   7

St Vincent parrot

C a r i b b e a n S e a

NICARAGUA

Keel-billed toucan

Swordfish

Clown fish

8

9

White-tail sabre wing hummingbird

PANAMA

Howler monkey

Spider monkey

0   1000km

0   500 miles

11

Rocky desert

The deserts of western USA are very dry and hot. Not many plants can grow in these harsh conditions. The animals that survive in this habitat have special ways of hunting and of protecting themselves from the fierce heat.

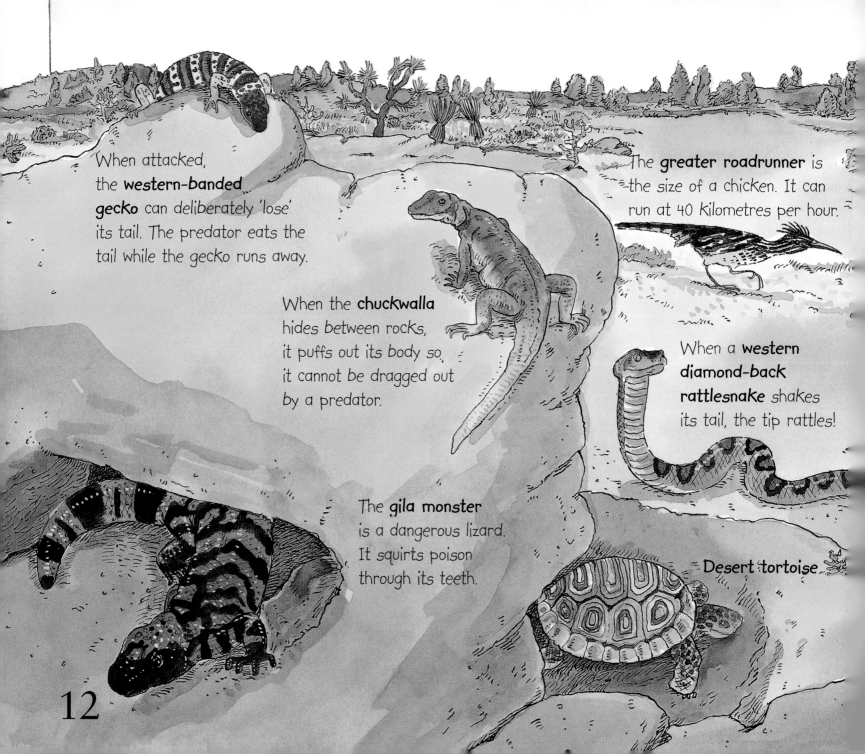

When attacked, the **western-banded gecko** can deliberately 'lose' its tail. The predator eats the tail while the gecko runs away.

When the **chuckwalla** hides between rocks, it puffs out its body so it cannot be dragged out by a predator.

The **greater roadrunner** is the size of a chicken. It can run at 40 kilometres per hour.

When a **western diamond-back rattlesnake** shakes its tail, the tip rattles!

The **gila monster** is a dangerous lizard. It squirts poison through its teeth.

Desert tortoise

The **red-tailed hawk** has excellent eyesight. It sees its prey moving a long distance away.

The **golden eagle** soars high above the desert, then swoops down at great speed to catch its prey.

The **mojave ground squirrel** sleeps in a burrow during the hottest months of the summer.

Painted lady butterfly

Mojave sooty-wing butterfly

Tarantula hawk wasp

The **desert rosy boa** is a snake that eats small animals and birds. It rolls up in a ball when attacked.

Rough harvester ants

Desert tarantula

13

EQUATOR

14

A   B   C   D

1   2   3

South America map with animals

COLOMBIA
VENEZUELA
GUYANA
SURINAM
FRENCH GUIANA (FRANCE)
ECUADOR
PERU
BRAZIL
BOLIVIA
PARAGUAY

Amazon
Amazon rainforest
Paraná
Andes Mountain

Galápagos Islands (Ecuador)

Scarlet ibis
Giant otter
Matamata turtle
Puma
Red howler monkey
South American bullfrog
Capybara
Fruit bat
Cavy
Poison dart frog
Black caiman
Jaguar
Harpy eagle
Toucan
Anaconda
Tapir
Blue morpho butterfly
Giant armadillo
Two-toed sloth
Maned wolf
Spectacled bear
Brown capuchin monkey
Andean condor
Chinchilla
Giant anteater
Galápagos giant tortoise

South America

South America has a variety of habitats. The Amazon rainforest contains more species than anywhere else on earth. The Andes, the world's longest mountain range, is home to many different animals. The southern grasslands are also rich in wildlife.

The **Andean condor** is one of the world's heaviest flying birds, weighing up to 11 kilograms. Amazingly, it can spot another condor 10 kilometres away.

Can you find one?

0		1000km
0	500 miles	

Atlantic Ocean

Pacific Ocean

ARGENTINA

URUGUAY

Sheep

Rhea

CHILE

Alpaca

Cattle

Pampas deer

Falkland Islands (UK)

Magellanic penguin

Sea lion

Fur seal

Sardines

15

4   5   6

A   B   C   D

Rainforest

The Amazon rainforest is very hot and also extremely wet – it rains for about 250 days a year. This combination is perfect for both plant and animal life, and this is why the rainforest is home to countless different species.

The colourful beak of the **toco toucan** is almost as big as the bird itself. It is mostly made of lightweight bone.

Blue morpho butterflies have bright blue wings. They flash when they catch the sunlight.

The **black caiman** is a big, dangerous alligator that preys on large animals, including humans.

Green iguana

Longhorn beetles have two antennae that can be longer than their bodies.

The steamy rainforest climate is ideal for frogs. The **poison dart frog** has bright colours to warn predators to keep away.

16

Scarlet macaw

Red howler monkeys

Tree kinkajou

The **two-toed sloth** eats, sleeps and even gives birth upside down!

Emerald tree boa

The world's largest rodent is the **capybara**. It is more than one metre long and 50 centimetres tall.

The spotted fur of the **jaguar** helps it hide in the shadows of the rainforest.

The strange **matamata turtle** snaps up small creatures as they float or swim by.

Giant otters can stay underwater for several minutes. Their sensitive whiskers help them find prey in the murky river.

17

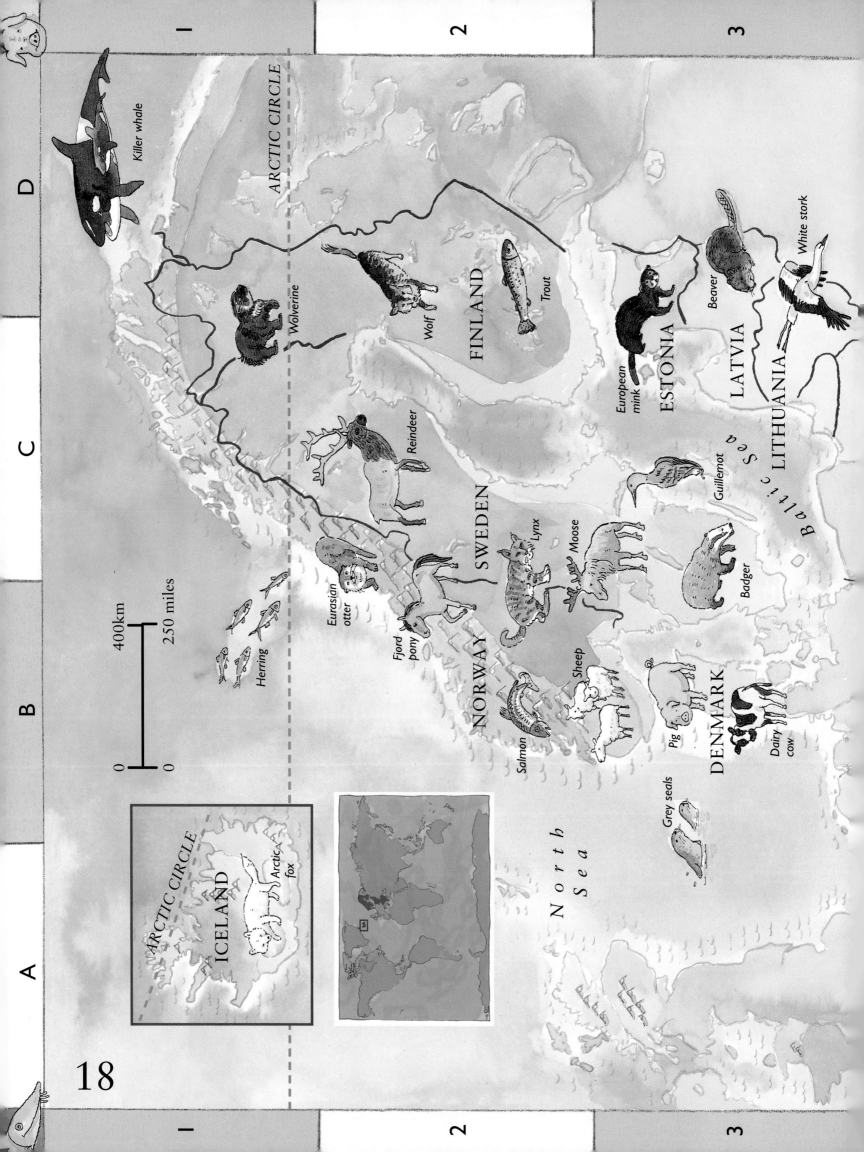

18

ARCTIC CIRCLE

Killer whale

FINLAND

Trout

Wolverine

Wolf

Beaver

European mink

ESTONIA

LATVIA

White stork

LITHUANIA

Baltic Sea

Reindeer

SWEDEN

Guillemot

400km

250 miles

Eurasian otter

Herring

Fjord pony

NORWAY

Lynx

Moose

Badger

Salmon

Sheep

Pig

DENMARK

Dairy cow

Grey seals

North Sea

ARCTIC CIRCLE

ICELAND

Arctic fox

Northern and eastern Europe

Animals that live in the north of Europe survive well in the cold, snowy pine forests and mountains. Further south, the climate is warmer and there is a greater variety of animal species. The wildlife that lives near the Mediterranean Sea is well suited to that hot climate.

The **reindeer** of northern parts of Norway and Sweden are always on the move in search of food. Large herds swim across freezing rivers and even through the sea between islands.

Can you find one on the map?

Vistula

Deer

European bison

CZECH REPUBLIC

POLAND

Muskrat

Tiger moth

Danube

SLOVAKIA

HUNGARY

Ibex

European hare

SLOVENIA

CROATIA

Heron

ROMANIA

Wild boar

Deer

BOSNIA & HERZEGOVINA

SERBIA & MONTENEGRO

Sturgeon

Garden dormouse

Danube

BULGARIA

Brown bear

Black Sea

ALBANIA

MACEDONIA

Lesser horseshoe bat

Goat

Marginated tortoise

GREECE

Bottlenose dolphin

Mediterranean Sea

A B C D

4 5 6

19

Western Europe

Europe is a small continent with many different animal habitats. Wildlife is found everywhere, from the cool, shady woodland to the hot, dry plains. Animals have also adapted to life in the high mountains of central and southern Europe.

Grey squirrels were brought to the UK from the USA in the 1800s. They are now more common than the smaller red squirrel.

Can you find one on the map?

Baltic Sea

Western European hedgehog

Brandt's bat

Avocet

NETHERLANDS

North Sea

Plaice

Cod

Highland cattle

Grey squirrel

Grey seal

SCOTLAND

UNITED KINGDOM

NORTHERN IRELAND

Sheep

WALES

ENGLAND

IRELAND

Horse

Haddock

A   B   C   D

1   2   3

4
5
6

D
C
B
A

GERMANY
White stork
Great white heron
Danube
European hare
Deer
BELGIUM
LUXEMBOURG
Wild boar
Rhine
Seine
Cow
FRANCE
Red fox
Atlantic Ocean
Loire
Brown crab
Oysters
Goose
Wild horse
ANDORRA
Griffon vulture
Ebro
Bull
Greater flamingo
SPAIN
PORTUGAL
Tagus
Apollo butterfly
Common genet
GIBRALTAR (UK)
Pilchards
Tuna
European lobster
21

AUSTRIA
LIECHTENSTEIN
Alps
Eurasian lynx
SWITZERLAND
Chamois
Ibex
Rhône
Po
Crested porcupine
SAN MARINO
ITALY
MONACO
Corsica (France)
Crayfish
Sardinia (Italy)
Bobtail squid
Sardines
White-spotted octopus
Balearic Islands (Spain)
Anchovies
Honey buzzard
Prawn
Swordfish
Sicily (Italy)
Mediterranean Sea
MALTA

Woodland

Trees that lose their leaves in winter are called 'deciduous'. Woods of deciduous trees, like this one in Europe, are home to many different animals, birds and insects. Each woodland creature has a special job to do, such as spreading seeds.

Long-eared bat

Only the male **blackbird** is black – the female is brown. Blackbirds eat insects, worms and berries.

Garden spider

Red admiral butterfly

Common shrew

The **adder** likes to bask in the sun in woodland clearings.

The **red fox** usually hunts at night. It eats nuts and berries as well as small forest creatures.

Earthworm

Green woodpecker

Tawny owl

In autumn, the **grey squirrel** buries food underground. It digs it up again in winter.

A **robin** fights other robins to protect its territory. It will even attack its own reflection!

Badger

The **garden snail** retreats into its shell when the weather is dry. It can then live for several months without water.

The **hedgehog** is usually active at night. During the day, it curls into a ball to sleep.

Wood mouse

Woodlice

23

Russia and its neighbours

Russia is a huge country, and the wildlife is
as varied as the landscape. Frozen tundra,
pine forests and mountain ranges are
home to many different creatures.
In countries south of Russia,
the climate is drier, and
tough animals survive
in the high-lying deserts.

Arctic Ocean

Collared lemming

Polar bear

Canada goose

Yenisey

Arctic cod

ARCTIC CIRCLE

Lynx

Moose

Ural Mountains

Reindeer

Golden eagle

Russian flying squirrel

Ob

KALININGRAD

Volga

Steppe polecat

Honeybee

Red fox

Snow leopard

BELARUS

Domestic pig

Ural

Wild boar

Saiga antelope

KAZAKHSTAN

UKRAINE

Chamois

Caspian seal

Bactrian camel

MOLDOVA

Black Sea

GEORGIA

Caspian Sea

UZBEKISTAN

KYRGYZSTAN

ARMENIA

Jackal

TAJIKISTAN

AZERBAIJAN

TURKMENISTAN

24

0   1000km

0   500 miles

Wolves live in pine forests. Their dark fur hides them in the shadows, helping them to catch prey.

Can you find one?

Beluga whale

Narwhal

Ringed seal

Snow goose

Walrus

Brown bear

S i b e r i a

Siberian deer

Siberian salamander

Bearded seal

Lena

Wolf

R U S S I A

Siberian hamster

Sea lion

Siberian tiger

A m u r

Pacific Ocean

Crested puffin

Sperm whale

25

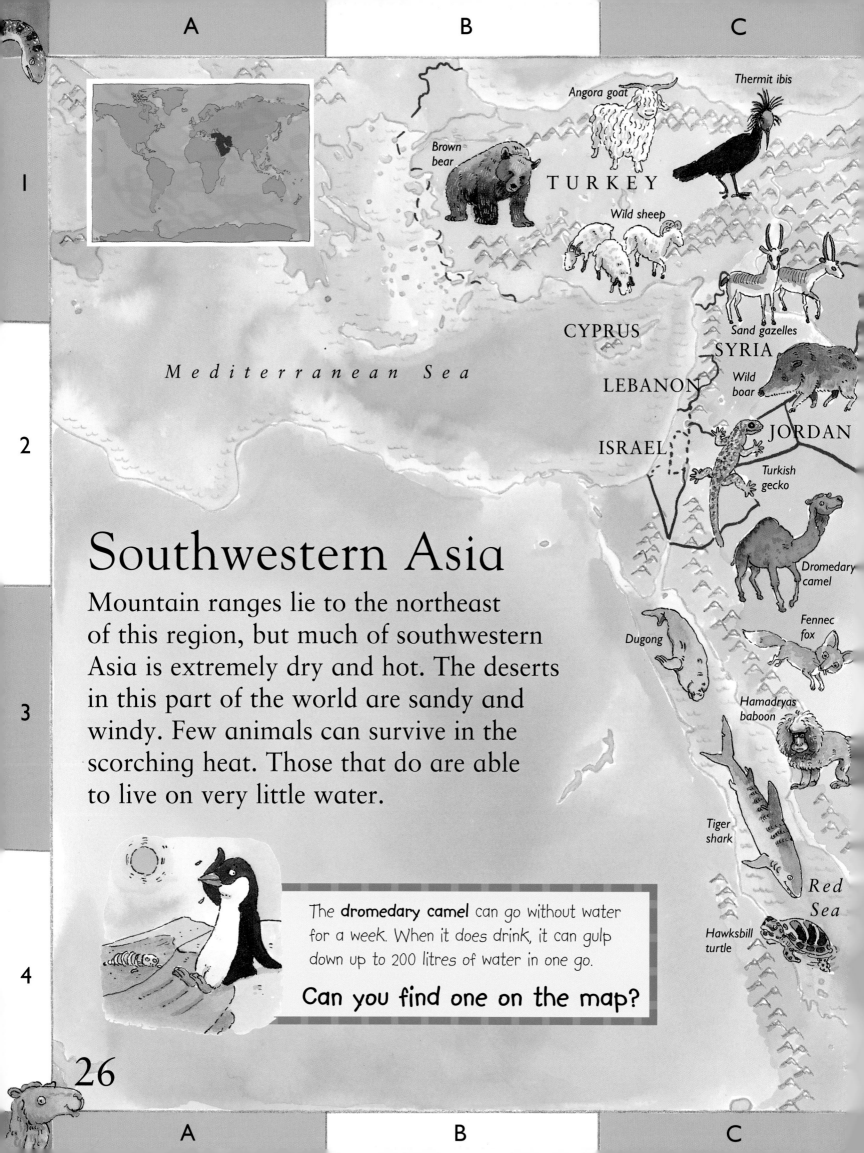

Brown bear

Angora goat

Thermit ibis

TURKEY

Wild sheep

CYPRUS

Sand gazelles

SYRIA

LEBANON

Wild boar

ISRAEL

Turkish gecko

JORDAN

M e d i t e r r a n e a n   S e a

Dromedary camel

Southwestern Asia

Dugong

Fennec fox

Mountain ranges lie to the northeast of this region, but much of southwestern Asia is extremely dry and hot. The deserts in this part of the world are sandy and windy. Few animals can survive in the scorching heat. Those that do are able to live on very little water.

Hamadryas baboon

Tiger shark

Red Sea

The **dromedary camel** can go without water for a week. When it does drink, it can gulp down up to 200 litres of water in one go.

Can you find one on the map?

Hawksbill turtle

D E F

0 800km

0 500 miles

1

Sturgeon

Southwest Asian spadefoot toad

Ant lion

Arabian mountain gazelle

IRAQ

Common crane

Rough-legged jerboa

Tiger beetle

IRAN

Iranian desert cobra

Tigris

Euphrates

Sand cat

Caracal

KUWAIT

Zagros Mountains

Persian ibex

2

Arabian Desert

Striped hyena

BAHRAIN

QATAR

OMAN

Iranian spiny-tailed lizard

SAUDI ARABIA

U.A.E.

Sardines

Death stalker scorpion

3

Arabian horse

OMAN

Lanner falcon

Wind scorpion

Arabian oryx

Manta ray

YEMEN

Large Aden gerbil

Arabian Sea

4

Veiled chameleon

Anchovies

Arabian angelfish

27

D E F

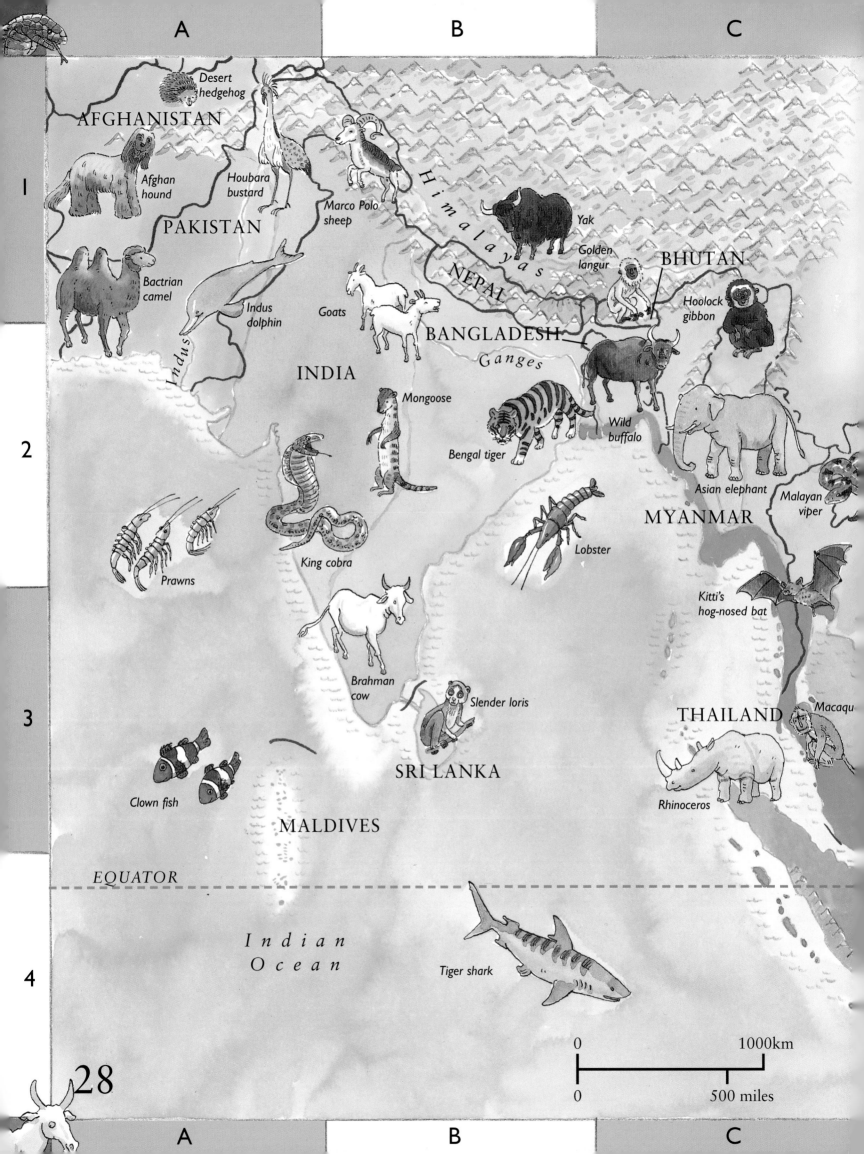

1

Desert hedgehog

AFGHANISTAN

Afghan hound

Houbara bustard

Marco Polo sheep

PAKISTAN

Bactrian camel

Indus dolphin

Indus

Goats

Himalayas

Yak

NEPAL

Golden langur

BHUTAN

Hoolock gibbon

BANGLADESH

Ganges

INDIA

Mongoose

Wild buffalo

Bengal tiger

Asian elephant

Malayan viper

MYANMAR

2

King cobra

Lobster

Prawns

Kitti's hog-nosed bat

Brahman cow

THAILAND

Slender loris

Macaqu

3

Clown fish

SRI LANKA

Rhinoceros

MALDIVES

EQUATOR

I n d i a n
O c e a n

Tiger shark

4

28

0   1000km

0   500 miles

Southern and southeastern Asia

A massive mountain range called the Himalayas lies to the north of this region. Countries south of the Himalayas are very hot, and those close to the Equator have a tropical climate. Much of Indonesia is covered with thick rainforest, which is home to a huge amount of wildlife.

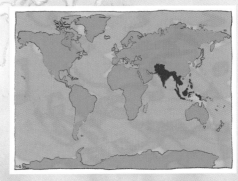

The **Komodo dragon** is the world's biggest lizard, and it looks like a living dinosaur. It grows up to three metres long.

Can you find one?

Asiatic black bear

VIETNAM

LAOS

Draco lizard

Clouded leopard

Manta ray

PHILIPPINES

CAMBODIA

MALAYSIA

SINGAPORE

Tarsier

Philippine cockatoo

BRUNEI

Hornbill

Giant palm civet

Pacific Ocean

Leatherback turtle

Orang-utan

I N D O N E S I A

Queen Alexandra birdwing butterfly

Malayan tapir

Komodo dragon

EAST TIMOR

29

The Himalayas

The Himalayas form the biggest range, or group, of mountains in the world. Fourteen of the world's tallest mountains are found in the Himalayas. The sturdy animals that live there are well adapted to life on the high slopes.

Musk deer

The **bharal** lives in small herds and is preyed on by snow leopards.

The **Himalayan brown bear** lives high up the mountain in summer, when it is not too cold to survive up there.

Himalayan weasel

Himalayan pika

When a male **rock agama** fights another male, he will try to hit the other lizard on the head with his tail!

30

The **bearded vulture** builds its nest high up on craggy mountain rocks. It feeds on dead animals, dropping the bones to smash them and get at the tasty marrow inside.

Red-billed blue magpie

Himalayan yellow-throated marten

The **yak** is a wild mountain ox. It climbs about 6,000 metres up the mountain to feed. An adult male can weigh as much as ten humans.

Marmot

Snow leopards can live higher up than any other wild cat. When they sleep, they wrap their tail around their body to keep warm.

Swallowtail butterfly

The male **Himalayan monal pheasant** is brightly coloured. The smaller female has no crest and is brown in colour.

31

Cattle

Mongolian sheep

MONGOLIA

Gobi Desert

Bactrian camel

Jerboa

Wild horse

Takla Makan Desert

CHINA

Vulture

Red panda

Plateau of Tibet

Cochin chickens

Tibetan antelope

Yak

Snow leopards

Giant panda

Chinese river dolphin

Water buffalo

Giant pandas live in the mountainous bamboo forests of western China. They spend at least 16 hours every day eating bamboo. In winter, their thick fur keeps them warm.

Can you find one on the map?

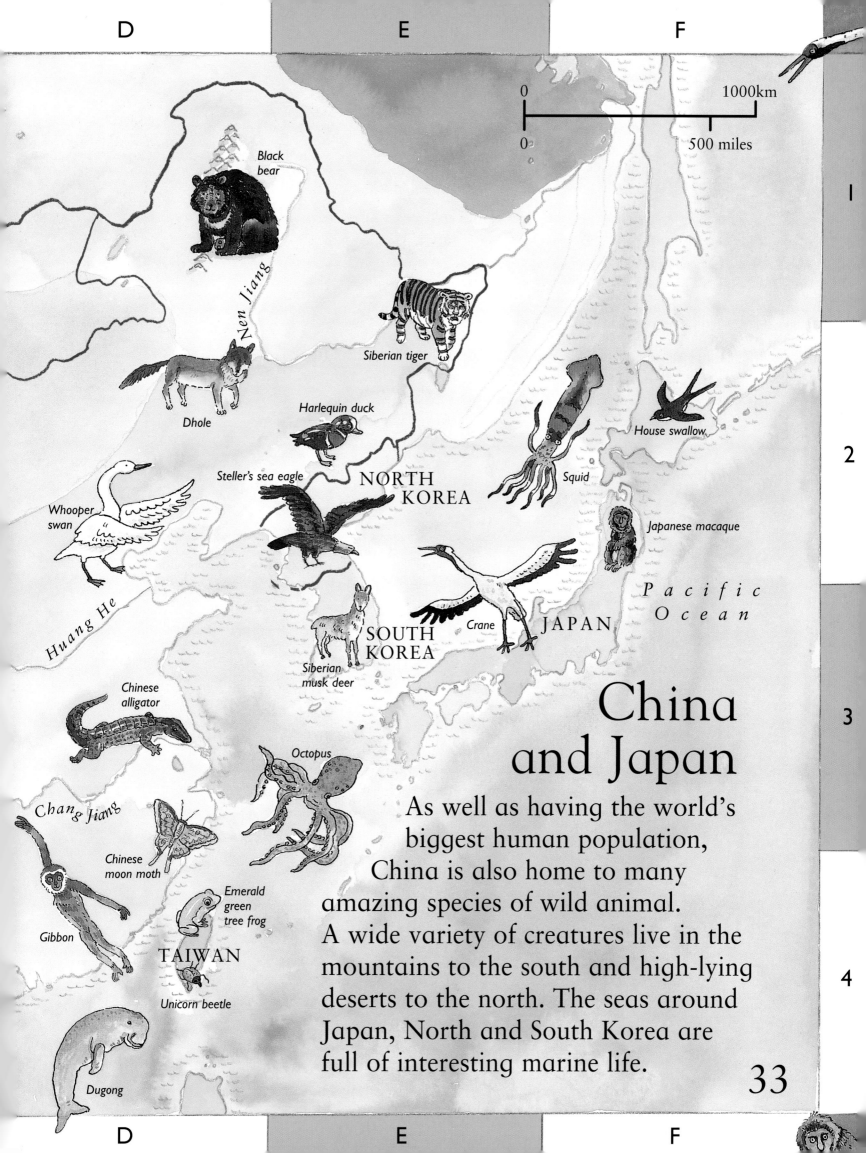

0   1000km

0   500 miles

Black bear

Nen Jiang

Siberian tiger

Dhole

Harlequin duck

House swallow

Steller's sea eagle

Squid

NORTH KOREA

Whooper swan

Japanese macaque

Huang He

Pacific Ocean

Crane

JAPAN

SOUTH KOREA

Siberian musk deer

Chinese alligator

China and Japan

Octopus

As well as having the world's biggest human population, China is also home to many amazing species of wild animal. A wide variety of creatures live in the mountains to the south and high-lying deserts to the north. The seas around Japan, North and South Korea are full of interesting marine life.

Chang Jiang

Chinese moon moth

Emerald green tree frog

Gibbon

TAIWAN

Unicorn beetle

Dugong

33

1

2

3

4

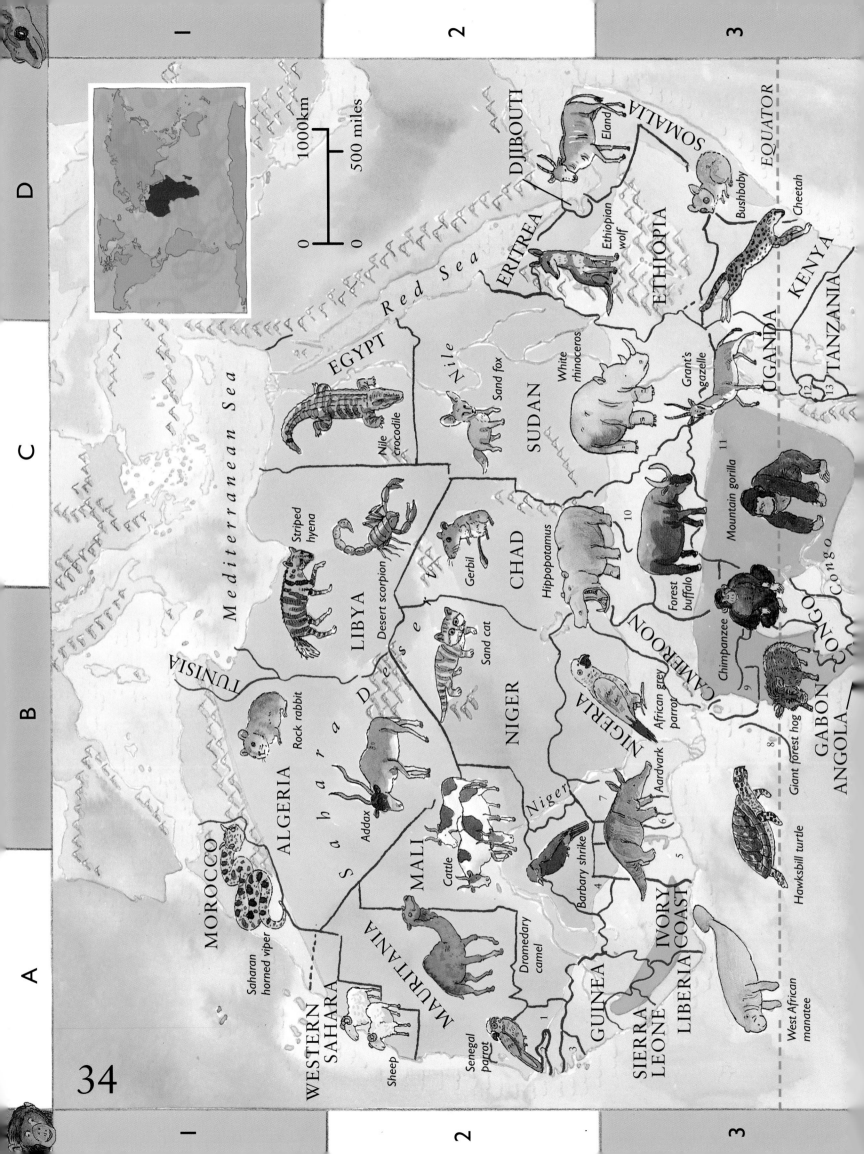

D   C   B   A

1   2   3

Sahara Desert

Mediterranean Sea

Red Sea

1000km
500 miles

MOROCCO

Saharan horned viper

WESTERN SAHARA

Sheep

MAURITANIA

Senegal parrot

MALI

Cattle

Dromedary camel

GUINEA

SIERRA LEONE

LIBERIA

IVORY COAST

West African manatee

Hawksbill turtle

Barbary shrike

Aardvark

Giant forest hog

African grey parrot

NIGERIA

CAMEROON

GABON

ANGOLA

CONGO

Congo

Chimpanzee

Mountain gorilla

Forest buffalo

Hippopotamus

CHAD

NIGER

Sand cat

Gerbil

Desert scorpion

Striped hyena

Rock rabbit

Addax

ALGERIA

TUNISIA

LIBYA

EGYPT

Nile crocodile

Nile

Sand fox

SUDAN

White rhinoceros

Grant's gazelle

UGANDA

KENYA

TANZANIA

Cheetah

Bushbaby

ETHIOPIA

Ethiopian wolf

ERITREA

DJIBOUTI

SOMALIA

Eland

EQUATOR

Niger

1   2   3   4   5   6   7   8   9   10   11   12   13

Africa

The enormous continent of Africa is home to a fantastic variety of wildlife. Some amazing animals live on grasslands south of the Sahara desert. In western Africa, tropical rainforests shelter many unusual and rare creatures. Further south, animals survive in dry bush land and hot desert.

Desert scorpions get all their water from food. They eat insects and spiders. Baby scorpions ride on their mother's back, underneath her deadly sting.

Can you find one on the map?

Key to African countries:

1 SENEGAL
2 GAMBIA
3 GUINEA-BISSAU
4 BURKINA FASO
5 GHANA
6 TOGO
7 BENIN
8 SÃO TOMÉ & PRÍNCIPE
9 EQUATORIAL GUINEA
10 CENTRAL AFRICAN REPUBLIC
11 DEMOCRATIC REPUBLIC OF CONGO
12 RWANDA
13 BURUNDI
14 MALAWI
15 ZIMBABWE

Atlantic Ocean

Indian Ocean

COMOROS

MADAGASCAR

MOZAMBIQUE

ZAMBIA

ANGOLA

NAMIBIA

BOTSWANA

SWAZILAND

LESOTHO

SOUTH AFRICA

African elephant

Ring-tailed lemur

Jackson's chameleon

Crested hornbill

Zambezi

Savanna baboon

Giraffe

Colobus monkey

Leopard

Kalahari lion

Zebra

Springbok

South African porcupine

Gecko

African wild dogs

Shrimps

Sardines

Herring

14

15

35

Savannah

The vast grassy plains of Africa are called 'savannah'. Herds of wild animals, such as gazelles, live in this habitat. They are hunted by lions and other faster, stronger animals.

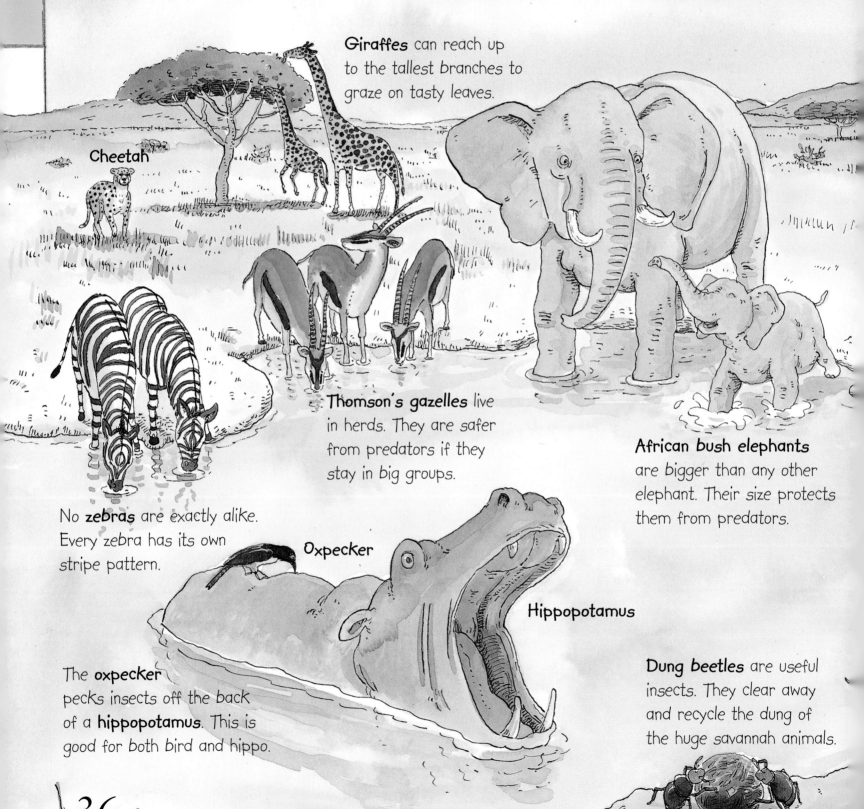

Giraffes can reach up to the tallest branches to graze on tasty leaves.

Cheetah

Thomson's gazelles live in herds. They are safer from predators if they stay in big groups.

No **zebras** are exactly alike. Every zebra has its own stripe pattern.

Oxpecker

Hippopotamus

African bush elephants are bigger than any other elephant. Their size protects them from predators.

The **oxpecker** pecks insects off the back of a **hippopotamus**. This is good for both bird and hippo.

Dung beetles are useful insects. They clear away and recycle the dung of the huge savannah animals.

Savannah *baboons*

The **griffon vulture** never kills its own food. It eats the meat of animals that are already dead.

Eastern black-white colobus monkeys shelter from the heat in the shady branches of a tree.

A male **lion** does not hunt as much as a female. Lions live in groups called prides.

If a **pangolin** is in danger, it rolls up into a *ball*.

Black rhinoceros come to waterholes to drink.

The **savannah monitor lizard** flicks its forked tongue to find prey. It eats birds, snakes, lizards and eggs.

The tusks of a male **warthog** can grow up to 63 centimetres long.

37

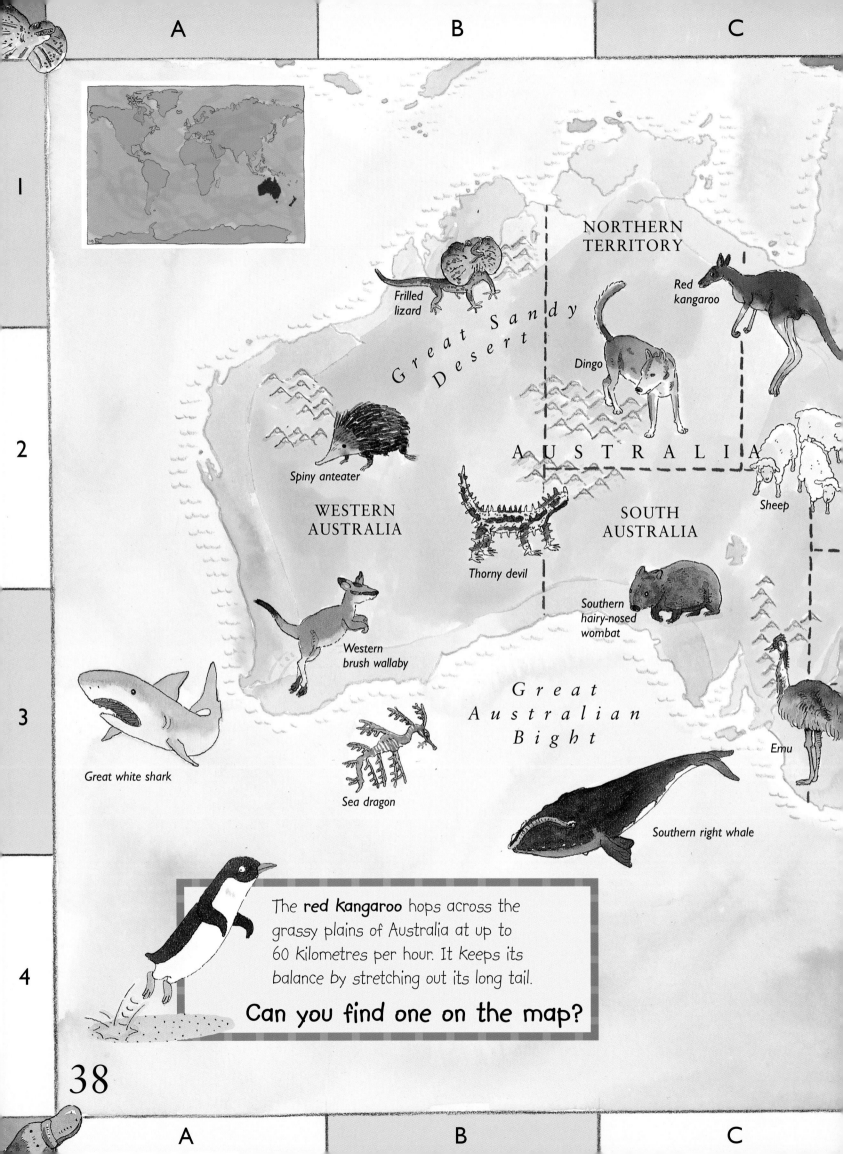

A B C

I

NORTHERN TERRITORY

Frilled lizard

Red kangaroo

Great Sandy Desert

Dingo

2

Spiny anteater

AUSTRALIA

WESTERN AUSTRALIA

SOUTH AUSTRALIA

Sheep

Thorny devil

Southern hairy-nosed wombat

Western brush wallaby

Great Australian Bight

3

Great white shark

Sea dragon

Emu

Southern right whale

The **red kangaroo** hops across the grassy plains of Australia at up to 60 Kilometres per hour. It keeps its balance by stretching out its long tail.

Can you find one on the map?

4

38

A B C

Australia and New Zealand

Some animals that live in this part of the world are not found anywhere else, such as the strange duck-billed platypus of Australia and the flightless kiwi of New Zealand. Animal farming is a big industry in Australia and New Zealand. There are many more sheep than people in both these countries.

Blacktip reef shark

Butterfly fish

Great Barrier Reef

Koala

Blue-ringed octopus

Duck-billed platypus

Great Dividing Range

QUEENSLAND

Darling

Kookaburra

NEW SOUTH WALES

Blue-tongued skink

Pacific Ocean

AUSTRALIAN CAPITAL TERRITORY

Murray

VICTORIA

T a s m a n S e a

Crown-of-thorns starfish

Scorpion fish

NORTH ISLAND

NEW ZEALAND

Long-tailed bat

Tasmanian devil

Kiwi

TASMANIA

SOUTH ISLAND

New Zealand sea lion

0   1000km

0   500 miles

The Pacific Islands

Thousands of tiny islands, home to lizards, birds and insects, are scattered across the South Pacific Ocean. The tropical waters are full of fascinating sea life.

Flying **fish** do not actually fly – they glide above the surface of the water on their outstretched fins.

Can you find one on the map?

Key to countries:
1 GUAM (USA)
2 PALAU
3 NAURU
4 WALLIS & FUTUNA ISLANDS (FRANCE)
5 TOKELAU (NZ)
6 SAMOA
7 AMERICAN SAMOA (USA)
8 NIUE (NZ)
9 COOK ISLANDS (NZ)
10 PITCAIRN ISLANDS (UK)

0   1000km

0   500 miles

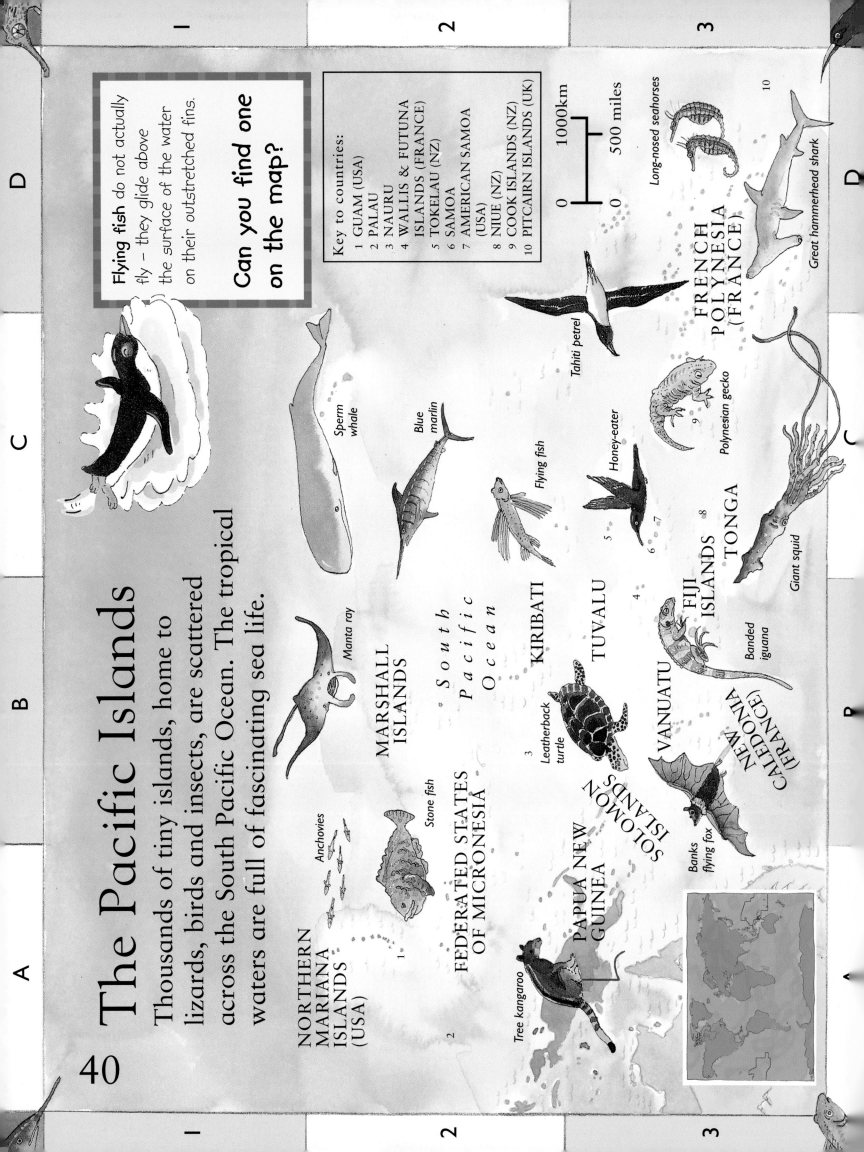

NORTHERN MARIANA ISLANDS (USA)

Anchovies

Stone fish

FEDERATED STATES OF MICRONESIA

MARSHALL ISLANDS

Manta ray

Sperm whale

Blue marlin

South Pacific Ocean

Flying fish

Honey-eater

Long-nosed seahorses

Tahiti petrel

FRENCH POLYNESIA (FRANCE)

Great hammerhead shark

Polynesian gecko

KIRIBATI

Leatherback turtle

TUVALU

VANUATU

FIJI ISLANDS

TONGA

Banded iguana

Giant squid

PAPUA NEW GUINEA

SOLOMON ISLANDS

NEW CALEDONIA (FRANCE)

Banks flying fox

Tree kangaroo

Coral reef

Coral reefs are formed with the shells of billions of tiny sea creatures. The Great Barrier Reef, which lies off the coast of northeast Australia, is home to a colourful collection of sea life.

The loggerhead turtle eats clams, crabs, jellyfish, squid and fish.

Spinner dolphins

Australian brain coral

Pygmy seahorses

Long-nosed butterfly fish

Sea urchin

Mandarin fish

Sea cucumber

Box jellyfish can grow as big as basketballs. They have a deadly sting.

Barrier reef anemonefish

Clown fish

Staghorn coral

The poisonous **olive sea snake** swims to the surface to breathe.

The poison of the **blue-ringed octopus** can kill an adult human in minutes.

Blue sea star

The **giant clam** is the world's largest mollusc. Its shell can be 1.5 metres long.

Blue-spotted fantail ray

Tubular sponge

41

The Arctic Circle

The frozen Arctic Ocean and the world's most northern lands are home to a surprising amount of wildlife. All Arctic creatures are specially adapted to life in this harsh habitat.

The **Arctic tern** migrates from the Arctic to Antarctica, then back again. It flies up to 40,000 kilometres in a single year.

Can you find one on the map?

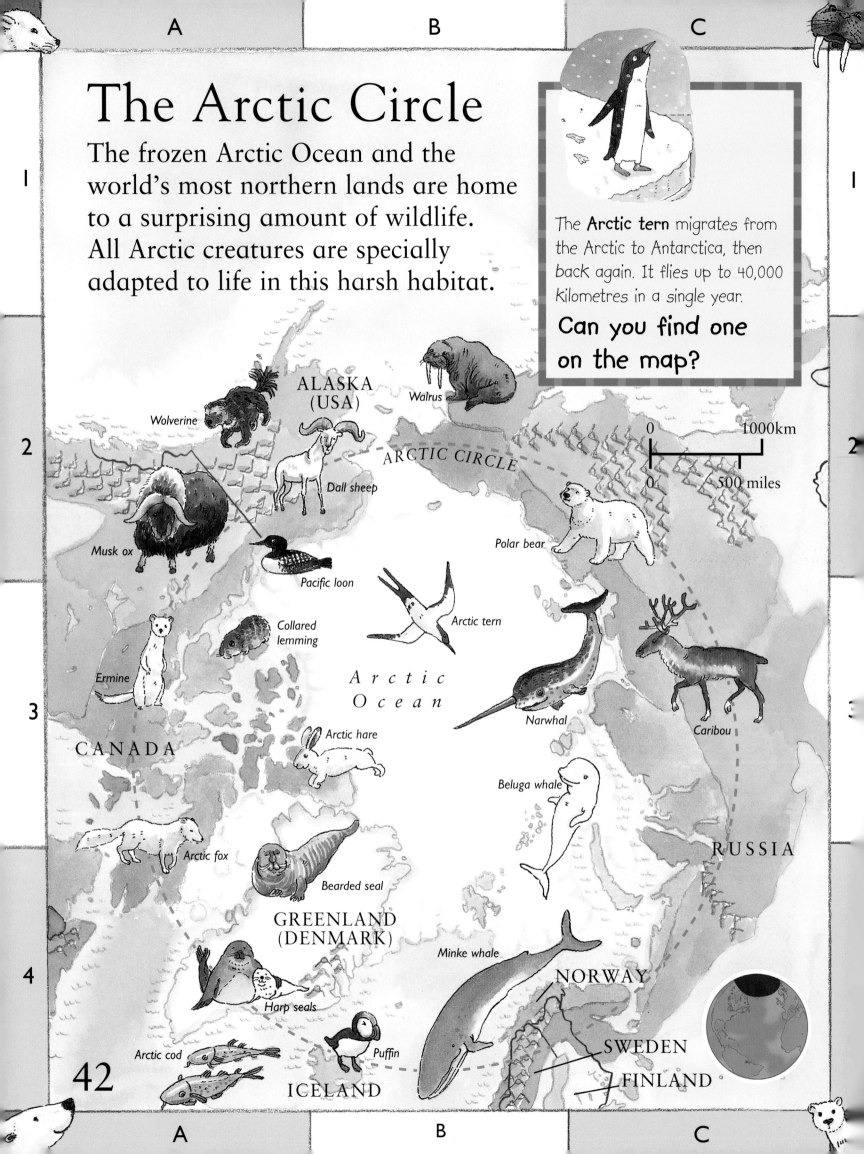

Wolverine

ALASKA (USA)

Walrus

Dall sheep

ARCTIC CIRCLE

0   1000km

0   500 miles

Musk ox

Pacific loon

Polar bear

Ermine

Collared lemming

Arctic tern

A r c t i c
O c e a n

Narwhal

Caribou

CANADA

Arctic hare

Beluga whale

RUSSIA

Arctic fox

Bearded seal

GREENLAND (DENMARK)

Minke whale

NORWAY

Harp seals

Arctic cod

Puffin

SWEDEN

FINLAND

ICELAND

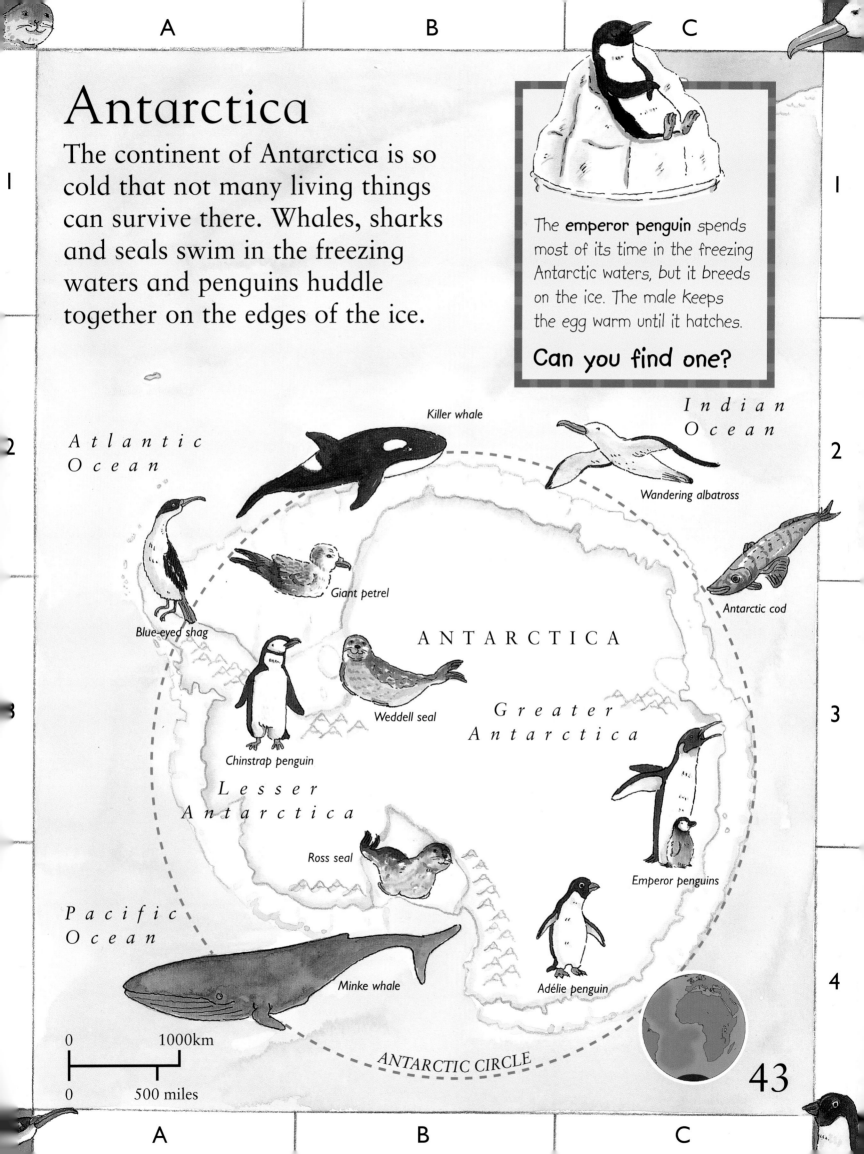

Antarctica

The continent of Antarctica is so cold that not many living things can survive there. Whales, sharks and seals swim in the freezing waters and penguins huddle together on the edges of the ice.

The **emperor penguin** spends most of its time in the freezing Antarctic waters, but it breeds on the ice. The male keeps the egg warm until it hatches.

Can you find one?

Killer whale

Indian Ocean

Atlantic Ocean

Wandering albatross

Giant petrel

Antarctic cod

Blue-eyed shag

ANTARCTICA

Weddell seal

Greater Antarctica

Chinstrap penguin

Lesser Antarctica

Ross seal

Emperor penguins

Pacific Ocean

Minke whale

Adélie penguin

0   1000km

0   500 miles

ANTARCTIC CIRCLE

43

The Arctic

Very few plants grow in the freezing lands of the Arctic. A treeless plain, called the tundra, stretches out in all directions. At the coast, icy seawater laps against bare rocks and ice. Arctic animals have developed clever ways to keep safe and warm in their cold environment.

The **narwhal** is a type of whale. Its tusk grows up to three metres long – about half the length of its body and tail.

Beluga whale

The **walrus** has long tusks that it hooks onto ice so it can sleep in water.

Ringed seals are the most common seals in the Arctic. They are hunted by polar bears.

Northern collared lemmings

Arctic terns have strong wings that measure up to 84 centimetres from tip to tip.

Unlike most owl species, the **snowy owl** is active in the day. Its legs and feet are covered in feathers to protect it from the cold.

Peary caribou

Arctic hares have white fur to help them hide in the snow.

The **arctic fox** shelters in a rocky den. Some dens have been used for centuries by generations of foxes.

A layer of fat under the fur of **polar bears** means they can swim in the sea without freezing to death.

45

Glossary

amphibian
An animal born in water that lives on land.

antenna (pl: antennae)
A feeler or horn.

burrow
A hole or tunnel where an animal lives.

climate
Usual weather in a place.

continent
One of earth's seven huge blocks of land.

coral reef
A living marine structure, formed with the shells of tiny sea creatures.

deciduous
A plant that loses its leaves in winter.

den
A sheltered place.

desert
A large area of dry land.

diet
Food that is usually eaten by a living thing.

dung
The body's waste.

environment
Natural surroundings.

Equator
An imaginary line around the middle of the earth.

fin
The thin, flat part of a fish's body.

flightless
Unable to fly.

glide
To fly without flapping.

graze
To eat grass or leaves.

habitat
An animal's home.

herd
A group of animals.

hibernate
To sleep all winter.

mammal
A warm-blooded animal that feeds its babies on milk.

marine
From the sea.

marrow
The soft insides of bones.

migration
Making the same journey at the same time every year.

mollusc
An animal with a soft body and hard shell.

plain
A flat, treeless area.

prairie
Flat grassland in North America.

predator
An animal that hunts and eats other animals.

prey
An animal that is hunted and eaten by another animal.

rainforest
Tropical forest with a hot, wet climate.

reptile
A cold-blooded animal that creeps or crawls.

rodent
An animal with big front teeth that it uses to chew.

school
A group of marine animals.

species
A set of animals or plants with the same features.

swamp
A marsh or bog.

tentacles
The long, bendy parts of an animal, used for gripping, feeling or moving.

territory
An area of land that belongs to an animal.

tropical
An area near the Equator with hot weather.

tundra
A treeless, frozen plain.

tusk
A long tooth that pokes out of an animal's mouth.

venom
Poison used to kill prey.

wingspan
The distance between wingtips.

Index